W9-CAD-967

Cornerstones of Freedom

The Story of
APOLLO 11

By R. Conrad Stein

Illustrated by David J. Catrow III

CHILDRENS PRESS ®
CHICAGO

Library of Congress Cataloging in Publication Data

Stein, R. Conrad.
    The story of Apollo 11.

    (Cornerstones of freedom)
    Summary: Highlights man's efforts to journey
to the moon, with a detailed account of the first
landing achieved by Apollo 11.
    1. Project Apollo—Juvenile literature.
[1. Project Apollo. 2. Space flight to the moon]
I. Title. II. Title: The story of Apollo eleven.
II. Series.
TL789.8.U6A58196   1985   629.45'4   85-10974
ISBN 0-516-04692-6   AACR2

"I believe this nation should commit itself to achieve the goal, before this decade is out, of landing a man on the moon and returning him safely to earth." So said President John F. Kennedy in an address to Congress on May 25, 1961. His words posed a challenge to the American people. At that time, American space efforts lagged far behind those of the Soviet Union. It took billions of dollars in tax money, plus the courage of dozens of astronauts and the intelligence and hard labor of hundreds of scientists and engineers, to narrow the Russian lead. But finally, eight years after Kennedy's speech, the first human visitor set foot on the moon. The event was hailed as the greatest achievement of the space age.

What is generally called the space age began on October 4, 1957. On that day, the Soviet Union rocketed into orbit around the earth a satellite that was about the size of a beach ball and weighed 184 pounds. A month later, the Russians launched

another artificial satellite. This one weighed an astonishing 1,120 pounds and carried a small dog named Laika. The two satellites speeding in endless loops far above the earth stunned scientists all over the world. No one had expected the Soviet Union to lead mankind into the space age. That honor was supposed to have gone to the United States, which had long been the world leader in science and technology.

At the time of the Russian launchings, American scientists were working on several projects designed to fire a satellite into earth orbit. The Americans, however, found the road to space to be filled with frustrations. Their rockets either failed to ignite, or exploded into colossal balls of fire while still on the launching pad. It was not until January, 1958, that the United States finally put an artificial satellite into orbit. And it weighed a mere thirty-one pounds. Subsequent American satellites were also tiny compared to the mammoth ones Russia fired aloft. This inequity prompted Soviet Premier Nikita Khrushchev to jeer, "You send up oranges while we send up tons."

A contest referred to as the "space race" developed between the United States and the Soviet Union. Many world leaders believed that this competition would have far-reaching consequences. They claimed that whichever political system led mankind into space would also dominate life here on earth.

Initially, all the prizes in the space race went to the Soviets. In September, 1959, Russian scientists launched a space probe that crashed into the moon. Less than a month later, another Russian space probe circled the moon and took photos of its far side, which had never before been seen by human beings. Finally, on April 12, 1961, Russian cosmonaut Yuri Gagarin was blasted into the sky to become the first man in space. Experts predicted that the Soviet Union would land men on the moon long before the United States, and the subsequent loss of prestige would be disastrous for America.

In America, a step-by-step manned space program made slow but steady progress. The program was headed by a government agency called the National Aeronautics and Space Administration (NASA). First, NASA launched two suborbital manned flights. Then, on February 20, 1962, Marine officer John Glenn blasted off in a tiny space capsule and became the first American to orbit the earth.

Between 1962 and 1966, NASA completed sixteen manned flights under programs called Mercury and Gemini. Those missions prepared astronauts for Project Apollo, which was designed to send a three-man crew to the moon. But tragedy soon struck the Apollo program.

On January 27, 1967, three astronauts climbed aboard an Apollo space capsule to perform some routine tests. The capsule sat atop a towering Saturn rocket. Suddenly, from inside the capsule, came a shout, "Fire in the spacecraft!" Another voice cried out, "Get us out of here!" A sheet of

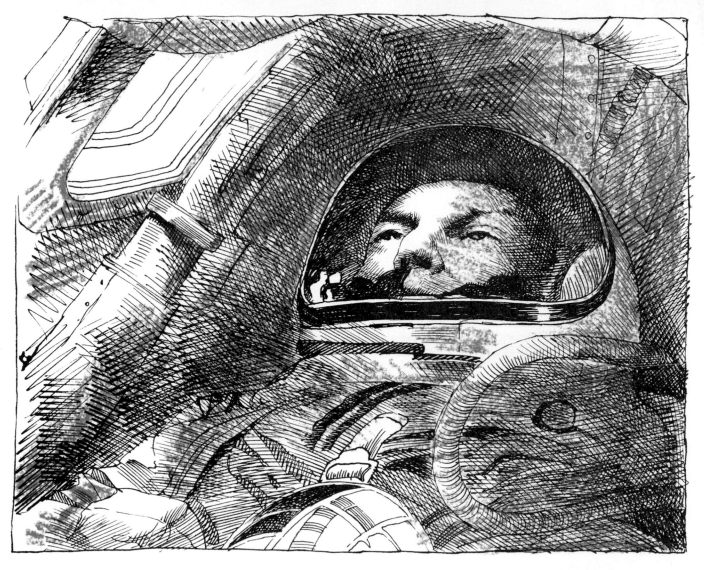

JOHN GLENN EARTH ORBIT, FEBRUARY 20, 1962

orange flame licked the inside of the craft's windows. Furiously, workers tried to open the hatches, but the intense heat drove them back. Three men inside—Virgil "Gus" Grissom, Edward White, and Roger Chaffee—died almost instantly from inhaling deadly smoke. A later investigation decided that a

short circuit probably caused a spark which led to the fatal fire.

The disaster caused a twenty-one-month delay in Project Apollo. Many safety features were added to the space capsule to prevent another horrible accident. As the work continued, NASA scientists and technicians recalled the words of Gus Grissom: "We are in a risky business, and we hope if anything happens to us it will not delay the program. The conquest of space is worth the risk of life."

On December 21, 1968, a preliminary flight called Apollo 8 rose from Cape Kennedy in Florida. It was destined for an orbit around the moon. Apollo 8's crew was made up of astronauts William Anders, James Lovell, and Frank Borman. To break away from the earth's gravitational pull, the craft had to reach the speed of 24,226 miles per hour. This was ten times faster than a rifle bullet, and far swifter than human beings ever had flown. While racing through the silent void of space, James Lovell looked back and saw his home planet. It floated like a blue and white marble suspended in an endless night. Lovell said, "When you see the earth slowly recede from you, there is a sensation in your stomach that is hard to describe."

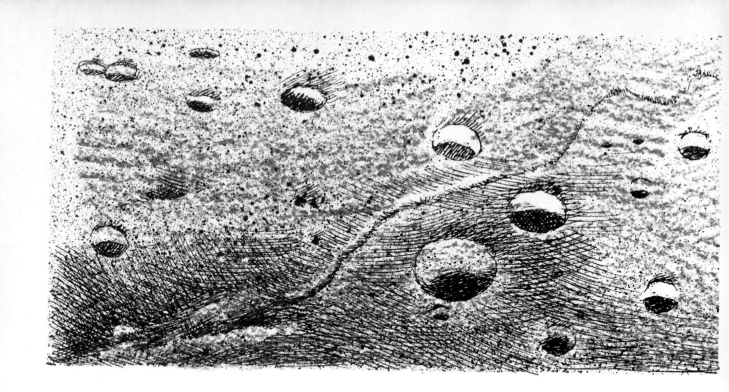

After three busy days in space, Apollo 8 achieved orbit around the moon. At one point, the spacecraft dipped as low as seventy miles above its surface. Awestruck, the men gazed down at the moon's tortured landscape. They saw broad wasted plains dotted by craters that looked like broken bubbles. "The vast loneliness of the moon is awe inspiring." said Lovell. Borman added that the moon is a "forbidding type of existence, a great expanse of nothing."

It was Christmas Eve, 1968, as the crew of Apollo 8 skimmed above the moon. They had sailed farther away from home than anyone had ever ventured before. Below them lay a stage of creation never

seen by human eyes. It is no wonder they chose to
read from the first page of the Bible as their
Christmas message to the world: "In the beginning
God created the heaven and the earth. And the earth
was without form. . .and darkness was on the face of
the deep. . . .And God said, Let there be light."

After Apollo 8, two more Apollo missions paved
the way for the historic moon landing. One mission,
Apollo 10, practiced every operation short of an
actual landing. It also dipped to within ten miles of
the moon. Meanwhile, an anxious world waited for
the flight of Apollo 11, and the incredible voyage
that would send American astronauts to the moon.

Since the dawn of man, the moon has been hailed as a silvery goddess of the night. The ancients both worshiped and feared her. To the Babylonians, the moon was the most powerful of the heavenly deities. To the Romans, she was Diana, goddess of the hunt and ruler of wild beasts. Nearly all peoples believed that the moon affected human behavior. It was once thought that falling asleep in moonlight would cause insanity. Even today some veteran policemen declare that the time of a full moon means an increase in violent crime.

For centuries, the moon was visited in the imagination of poets and dreamers. Writing shortly after the time of Christ, the Greek Lucian told of a hero whose ship was lifted out of the sea and propelled to the moon by a colossal waterspout. In a story written in the 1600s by Englishman Francis Godwin, a man was flown to the moon by a team of magical swans. Characters created by the great French writer Jules Verne were fired to the moon out of a giant cannon. Moon flight was a common theme in twentieth-century comic books and science-fiction stories for many decades prior to the actual accomplishment.

Few things are more exciting than fantasies com-

ing true. The flight of Apollo 11 became much more than one nation's expedition to the earth's ancient companion. Instead, it was looked upon as mankind's greatest adventure.

On launching day, a Saturn rocket stood steaming on its pad at Cape Kennedy. It was the largest, most powerful machine ever made. The rocket, topped by the spacecraft, towered as high as a thirty-five story building. It was heavier than the combined weight of twenty-five jet liners. Five million separate parts built by 300,000 workers had gone into its construction. The work had involved tons of blueprints, millions of manual pages, and contracts from twenty thousand different companies. The Apollo 11 spacecraft itself had three basic parts: a command module (the *Columbia*), a lunar module (the *Eagle*), and a service module. At blast-off, the mighty rocket engine would burn fifteen tons of fuel a second. All this to send to the moon a vehicle that weighed about as much as a hefty pickup truck.

Never before had so many millions of people been eyewitnesses to history. In addition to American television, radio, and print media, the Apollo 11 launch was covered by 850 foreign journalists representing fifty-five countries and speaking thirty-three different languages. As United States President Richard Nixon said, "Today the miracles of space travel are matched by miracles of space communication. Even across the vast lunar distance, television brings the moment of discovery into our homes and makes us all participants."

The moment the world had waited for came at 9:32 A.M. on July 16, 1969. "Ten, nine, eight, seven, six, five, four, three, two, one, zero...lift-off. We have a lift-off!" Riding on top of a thundering pillar of fire, the Saturn rocket and Apollo 11 rose magnificently into the sky. The great adventure had begun.

In the spacecraft were astronauts Neil Armstrong, Edwin "Buzz" Aldrin, Jr., and Michael Collins. Neil Armstrong commanded the mission, and was scheduled to be the first man to set foot on the moon. He knew the people on earth expected him to make some sort of dramatic statement when he made the first human footprint in the moon's dust. Days earlier, Armstrong had decided what words he would say, but he refused to give reporters even a hint of what they would be.

Navigators on earth kept a close watch on Apollo 11's course. The moon, in its orbit around the earth,

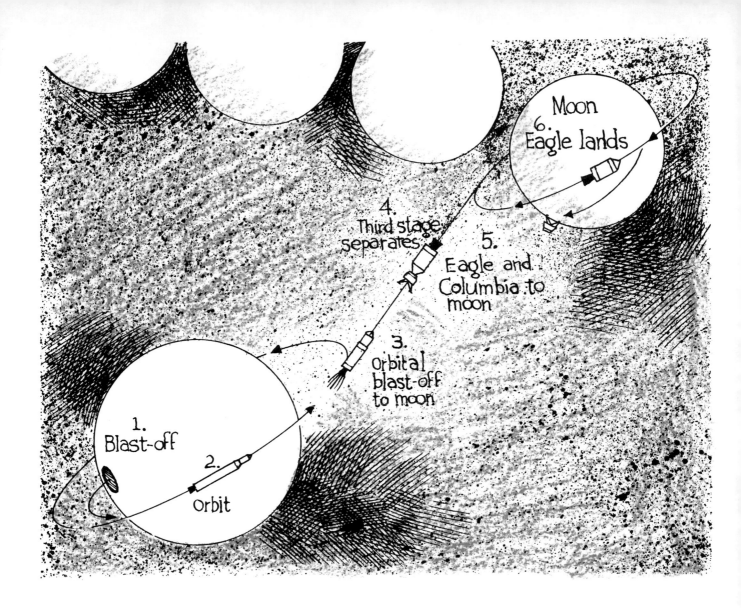

is constantly moving at high speed. Trying to intercept it with a spacecraft can be compared to throwing a stone into the air and then hitting it in midflight with another stone. Apollo 11 had to be aimed at a point far ahead of the moon's path, and then fly at a precise speed to reach that point at the same time the moon did.

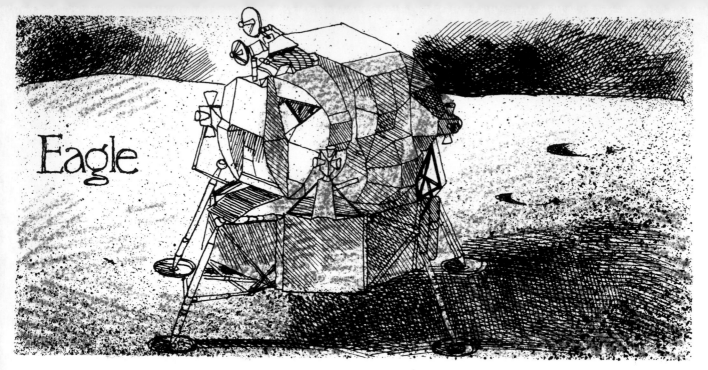

Eagle

Aided by Mission Control at the Houston Space Center, the second stage of the Saturn rocket was released and the third stage ignited. Apollo 11 achieved a lunar orbit precisely on schedule. Neil Armstrong and Buzz Aldrin prepared to pilot the *Eagle* to a moon landing while Michael Collins would remain aboard the *Columbia.* When all was ready, the two spaceships separated and moved silently along different paths. Neil Armstrong radioed back to Houston, "The *Eagle* has wings."

The *Eagle* was a clumsy-looking vehicle that lacked space-age streamlining. It resembled a four-legged spider riding an invisible thread. But in the airless void, the *Eagle* had no need for the niceties of smooth design. Down, down, down it plunged, edging ever closer to history.

Then Neil Armstrong strained to look out the porthole and noticed potential disaster. The *Eagle* was dropping toward a rugged wasteland strewn with giant boulders. Coolly, Armstrong searched for a level spot on the jagged surface. He was the most skilled of the three pilot-astronauts, and one of the finest pilots in all the world. He spotted a likely area, but he knew that maneuvering of any kind required the burning of fuel. Fuel was the most precious substance aboard the *Eagle.* Still, Armstrong fired the rocket engine to slow the descent and steer the craft toward the level plain.

At Mission Control in Houston, technicians watched and worried as instruments showed the *Eagle's* fuel reaching a dangerously low point. Finally, with only 5 percent of the fuel remaining, a light blinked on the instrument panel indicating that Armstrong had landed the vehicle safely. The Houston Space Center radioed the men on the moon, "You got a bunch of guys about to turn blue. We're breathing again. Thanks a lot."

The millions of viewers on earth were not aware that the spacecraft had been in such peril. They heard only Armstrong's historic report, "The *Eagle* has landed." It was Sunday, July 20, 1969.

After instruments were checked and the astronauts had squeezed into their $300,000 space suits, all was ready for the first moon walk. Armstrong opened the hatch and began a slow descent of the ladder. On the second step, he pulled a cord to activate a television camera that was pointed at him. Suddenly, the world was treated to a picture of Armstrong's ghostly figure edging downward with the moon's forbidding landscape in the background. A caption underneath the television picture read: LIVE FROM THE MOON. It was later estimated that one of every four people on earth watched this history-making event or followed it on the radio.

Near the bottom, Armstrong told Houston, "I'm at the foot of the ladder. The [*Eagle's*] footpads are only depressed in the surface about one or two inches, although the surface appears to be very, very fine grained as you get close to it. I'm going to step off. . .now." This was the moment half a billion people had waited to see. As his foot touched the timeless dust of the moon, Armstrong said, "That's one small step for a man, one giant leap for mankind."

In millions of homes around the world, awed tele-

vision viewers exclaimed, "He did it!" "A man is actually on the moon!" "Fantastic!" "Unbelievable!"

Timidly at first, Armstrong paced about this strange and alien world almost a quarter of a million miles from his home. "The surface is fine and powdery. I can—I can pick it up loosely with my toe....I only go in a small fraction of an inch, maybe an eighth of an inch, but I can see the footprints of my boots and the treads in the fine sandy particles." Nineteen minutes after Armstrong's descent, Buzz

Aldrin stepped down the ladder and joined his commander. In contrast to the desolate world seen by Apollo 8's crew, Aldrin was impressed by a strange loveliness on the moon's rugged face. "It has a stark beauty all its own," he told Houston. "It's like much of the high desert in the United States. It's different, but it's very pretty out here."

Because the moon has only one sixth of earth's gravity, the men found walking to be a peculiar adventure at first. But in some ways the reduced

gravity was a blessing. The bulky packs carried by Armstrong and Aldrin weighed some five hundred pounds back on earth. On the moon, however, those same packs weighed less than one hundred pounds each. The astronauts quickly discovered that the easiest way to move about was to hop on both feet like kangaroos.

The men kept to a busy schedule. They put up a stainless steel plaque that read: "Here men from planet Earth first set foot on the moon, July, 1969, A.D. We came in peace for all mankind." Near the plaque they placed a shoulder patch of the Apollo 1 mission, whose crew had been killed in the tragic fire. They also left medals commemorating two Soviet cosmonauts who had died in their country's space efforts. They planted an American flag in the lunar soil, and Aldrin stiffly saluted it. Finally, the two men received the longest long-distance phone call in history. From Washington, President Nixon told them, "For one priceless moment in the whole history of man, all the people of this earth are truly one. One in their pride in what you have done, and one in our prayers that you return safely to earth."

The astronauts devoted most of their time to chores given them by scientists. They gathered

about fifty pounds of moon rocks to take home. They recorded surface temperatures: 234 degrees above zero Fahrenheit in the sun, and 279 degrees below zero in the shade. They assembled a special seismometer to measure the strength of "moon-quakes" and radio that information to scientists on earth.

After two hours, Houston radioed the men, "It's about time for you to start your close-out activities." Neil Armstrong said he wanted to gather more moon rocks. But, in a tone of voice that sounded like an impatient father, Houston said, "Neil and Buzz. Let's press on. . . .We're running a little low on time."

When the two astronauts were back aboard the *Eagle*, the world waited nervously for the second lift-off. An unstated question burned in the mind of nearly every television viewer: What would happen if the engine failed to work and the men could not take off? The answer: Armstrong and Aldrin would die on the moon when their oxygen supplies ran out. Rescue was impossible.

But the lift-off from the moon was flawless. Soon the *Eagle* docked with the *Columbia*. Armstrong and Aldrin rejoined their shipmate Michael Collins, the forgotten man of the first moon walk. After the docking, Houston said, "You're looking great. It's been a mighty fine day." Collins replied, "Boy, you're not kidding."

Back on earth all the world hailed the men as heroes, but there were no hugs and kisses. Immediately after splashdown, the astronauts were hurried into special isolation quarters. Scientists feared that there might be bacteria on the moon that would prove deadly if brought back to earth. A thorough examination, lasting several days, revealed no bacteria. The men were released from isolation, and given the heroes' welcome they deserved.

Apollo 11 was the first of six lunar landings conducted by NASA between 1969 and 1972. One mission, Apollo 13, launched in April of 1970, almost ended in tragedy when an explosion forced the crew to abort their moon landing and return to earth. Moon walks on later missions were much longer in duration and covered far more territory than did the ones taken by Armstrong and Aldrin. A few astronauts even rode about in a specially designed moon-roving car. All told, Apollo's six crews brought back to earth 841 pounds of moon rock and soil. To scientists, this material was more priceless than gold. Some one thousand scientists from nineteen different countries studied the samples and learned much about earth's cosmic neighbor.

Today, the goals remaining for space exploration are as limitless as the stars in the sky. Since 1972, there have been no spaceflights as spectacular as the moon landings, but the great space adventure is not over. Some day a man or woman from planet Earth will set foot upon the surface of Mars. When that happens, the drama of Apollo 11—the spaceflight that electrified the world—will be relived once more.

About the Author

R. Conrad Stein was born and grew up in Chicago. He enlisted in the Marine Corps at the age of eighteen and served for three years. He then attended the University of Illinois where he received a bachelor's degree in history. He later studied in Mexico, earning an advanced degree from the University of Guanajuato. Mr. Stein is the author of many other books, articles, and short stories written for young people.

Mr. Stein now lives in Chicago with his wife, Deborah Kent, who is also a writer of books for young readers, and their daughter Janna.

About the Artist

David J. Catrow III was born in Virginia and grew up in Hudson, Ohio. He spent three years in the United States Navy as a hospital corpsman and subsequently attended Kent State University, where he majored in biology. He is a self-taught illustrator. Mr. Catrow currently lives in Springfield, Ohio with his wife Deborah Ann and children Hillary and D.J. He is an editorial cartoonist for the *Springfield New-Sun*. The artist would like to thank his wife Deborah for her constant support and inspiration.